I Pledge Allegiance to the Flag

By Kathy Patterson

AuthorHouse™
1663 Liberty Drive
Bloomington, IN 47403
www.authorhouse.com
Phone: 1-800-839-8640

First published by AuthorHouse 08/16/2011

ISBN: 978-1-4567-2816-8 (sc)

Library of Congress Control Number: 2011902937

Printed in the United States of America

I Pledge Allegiance to the Flag

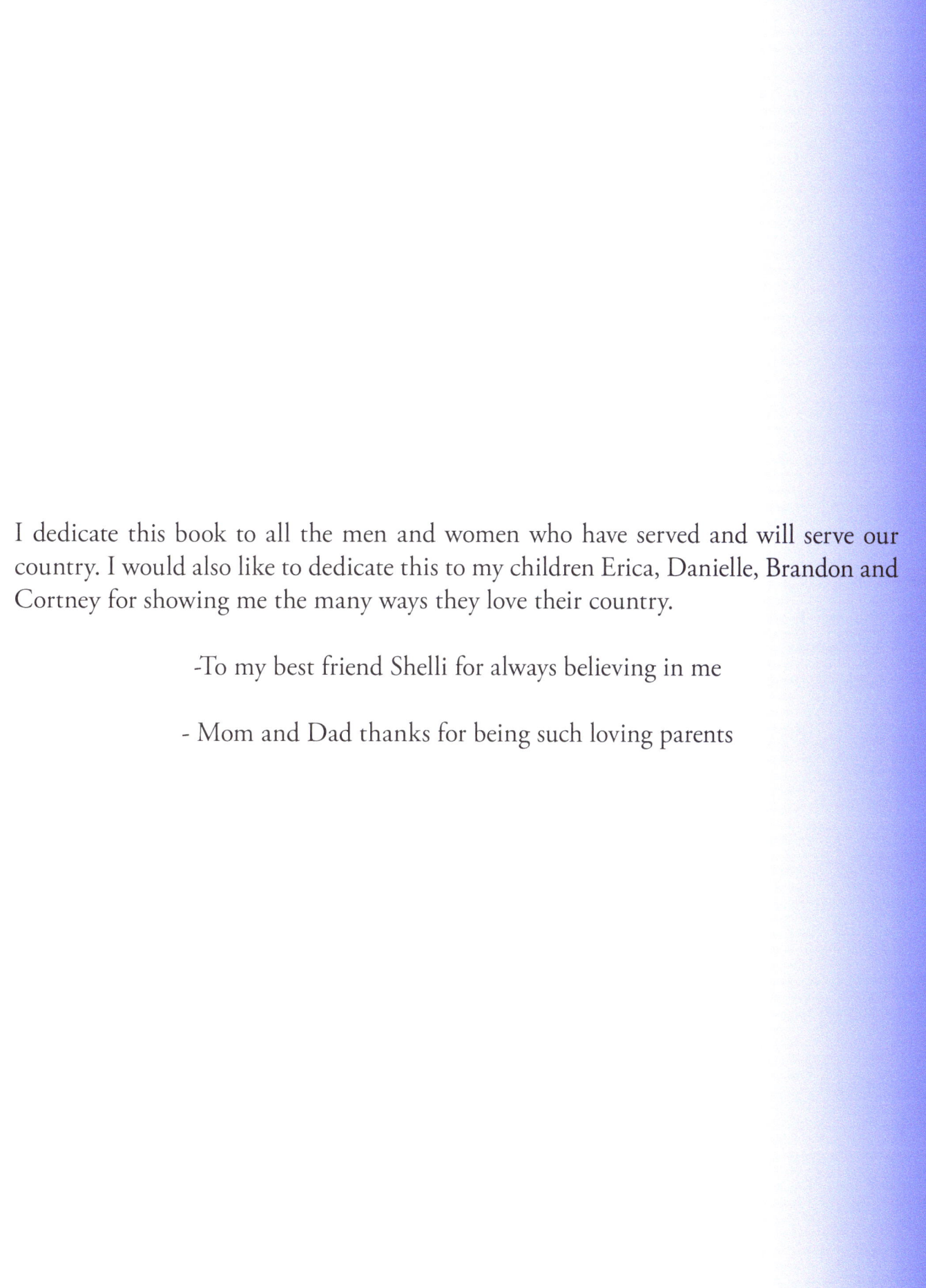

I dedicate this book to all the men and women who have served and will serve our country. I would also like to dedicate this to my children Erica, Danielle, Brandon and Cortney for showing me the many ways they love their country.

-To my best friend Shelli for always believing in me

- Mom and Dad thanks for being such loving parents

Dear Reader:

Since I was five years old I have recited the Pledge of Allegiance a countless number of times. However, it was not until I was in high school that I understood what the Pledge of Allegiance meant, and not until 9/11 that I understood what the Pledge meant to me. The United States was under attack, and we needed our forces now more than ever. Many people were called to immediate duty. That was the day in America that I saw my fellow people come together as one. We were united, and we stood as one. Indivisible.

I remember walking down the street in my hometown speaking to strangers like we were family, and watching Americans helping other Americans through such a horrific time. We were one, we were united. So many brave people went to the site with one thing in mind: "What can I do to help?" I saw the Pledge of Allegiance in action- we, the people, were a living pledge. It was no longer simply words on paper that I had recited for so many years. It was a real, living pledge to my country and the people in my country. **Allegiance. (Loyalty, devoted to helping others in time of need).**

In the days that followed people flew from around the country to Ground Zero to help. People were knitting booties for dogs so they could search for survivors. Some people sent money while others were planning fundraisers to help raise money for the American Red Cross. **Pledge (Americans promising each other that they will be there when their fellow Americans need them).**

Many looked to our leader for guidance. It did not matter what political party we had supported in the past - our leader was our leader and we needed to come together as a country to support the decisions that needed to be made.

I am a fourth grade teacher and I wanted my students to see the Pledge of Allegiance through the eyes of others. I asked community members to write up what the Pledge of Allegiance means to them. The first set of quotes was from local veterans. Their words were so powerful. I then asked students, teachers, and many others for their quotes, and I was truly amazed with their sincerity.

It is now that I teach my students that the Pledge of Allegiance is not just words written on paper. It is who we are as citizens of this country, and the actions we, the people, choose on a daily basis. Thank-you veterans, teachers, students, and community members for reminding me how lucky I am to be part of such a great country.

"I pledge allegiance to the flag..."

What it means to me...

Robert Herman

U.S. Air Force Korea

"The Pledge of Allegiance pays honor to the flag of our country."
To leave this country during a war period is to protect the freedom we have today.

John McMahon

U.S. Army WWII

"The Pledge of Allegiance means to me, I would lay down my life to preserve
this great country. The pledge does not wear out."

Kevin Eldred

Student Grade 8

"It means to pay our respects for our freedom."

What It Means

Pledge- A promise

Allegiance-Loyalty, devotion

Flag- Symbol for our country

Fun Facts

Story of Our Pledge

In 1892, Francis Bellamy, a Baptist minister, was in charge of preparing a program for the public schools quadricentennial celebration for Columbus Day. He planned a flag raising ceremony with a flag salute. This flag salute today is known as "The Pledge of Allegiance". Francis Bellamy's original Pledge "I Pledge allegiance to my flag and the Republic for which it stands, one nation, indivisible, with liberty and justice for all."

"Of the United States of America..."

What it means to me...

Edson Thomas Jr.

U.S. Army Vietnam

"Every time I say the Pledge it reminds me of Vietnam, the symbol we fought under was the flag, it kept us sane. It was the only thing that kept us sane."

Dani Lunn

Student Support Center Coordinator

"When I recite the Pledge I am reminded of what a great nation the US is, and I am recommitted to my love of and loyalty to my country. What a great way to begin each day!"

Mercedes Belanger

Student Grade 8

"It means that our country is independent and free. It means we are one. I think it is a way of showing we are true to our country when we say it."

Tucker Huntoon

Student Grade 8

"To me the Pledge means that lots of people care about our country."

What It Means

United States of America-The name of our country

Fun Facts

Story of Our Pledge

Against Mr. Bellamy's protest, the National Flag conference in 1923, and 1924 changed the Pledge's words, "my flag" to "the Flag of the United States of America."

After World War II, Congress voted to add the words "under God" to the Pledge.

In 1942, Congress made the pledge to the flag the official Pledge to the American flag.

"And to the Republic for which it stands..."

What it means to me...

David Tellman

U.S. Army Korea

"The Pledge of Allegiance is first to the flag of the United States of America, but a flag is only a symbol. For me the words "and to the republic for which it stands" represent the true meaning of the Pledge. Each time we say these words we are expressing our support of our nation, its constitution, its laws and the liberties, freedom and the responsibilities we share with all our fellow citizens to keep our nation free and strong."

Martha Hardiman

Middle School Language Arts Teacher

"It is a symbol of honor and respect for democracy and our country in particular. Furthermore, it honors all the men and women who have fought in the past (and will fight in the future) to keep our country free."

Nancy Annunziato

Elementary Language Arts Teacher

"Taking a moment to acknowledge my love and respect for my country."

Jerry Chelle

U.S. Navy Vietnam

"To honor the values of our forefathers"

What It Means

Republic- A kind of government where people vote and elect their leaders

Fun Facts

Story of our Pledge

Today, some Americans would like to change the words of the Pledge. Here is one version without the phrase "under God".

"I pledge allegiance to my Flag, and to the Republic for which it stands, one nation, indivisible, with equality, liberty and justice for all."

"One nation under God, indivisible,
with liberty and justice for all."

What it means to me…

Joe Barron

Student Grade 8

"The Pledge is important to me. It reminds me of how many people have died to honor our country. To me, the Pledge is to honor them."

Stanley Glines U.S. Navy

WWII

"The Pledge of Allegiance to our flag means I have Faith in my country because the flag represents the United States of America."

Nicole Bell Teacher

Grade 4

"The Pledge reminds me every day to remember all the great men and women who protect our country. It reminds me to be a better person."

Heather Stewart

ESL Teacher

"I am reminded of our national history, and the ideals of the United States government after important events like the Civil War."

What It Means

Nation – Another word for country

Indivisible – Something that cannot be pulled apart

Liberty – Freedom

Justice – Means fair

Fun Facts

American Flag Symbols

The 13 stripes stand for the original 13 colonies

Red- bravery

White- purity

Blue-justice

Stars- represent the states

In 1959, Alaska and Hawaii became states. The flag added two stars for these new states, the same number as today.

Respecting Our Flag

The Pledge of Allegiance and the National Anthem

The pledge of allegiance should be rendered by standing at attention, facing the flag and saluting. When the national anthem is played or sung, citizens should stand at attention and salute at the first note and hold the salute through the last note. The salute is directed to the flag, if displayed, otherwise to the music.

Parading and Saluting the Flag

When carried in a procession, the flag should be to the right of the marchers. When other flags are carried, the flag of the United States may be centered in front of the others or carried to their right. When the flag passes in a procession, or when it is hoisted or lowered, all should face the flag and salute.

Respecting the Men and Women Who Serve Our Country

What you can do for veterans and men and women serving our country:

- On Veteran's Day thank and honor all those who served in the military.

- Draw a picture about how you honor veterans.

- Have your school make a poster with the names and pictures of your local community members who are veterans.

- Invite veterans to your classroom.

- Discuss Veteran's Day and what it means to you and your family.

- During a parade when veterans, men and women in the service, or our flag pass by, put your hand over your heart.

- Make cards to thank veterans, and then send them to a local VA Hospital.

- Make cards and send them to a squadron/battalion.

- Make a bulletin board in your school with members from your community serving our country.

- Send cards to family members of a serving soldier.

These small random acts of kindness that we offer to those who serve our country are so vital to our living pledge.

Star Spangled Banner

Oh, say, can you see, by the dawn's early light,
What so proudly we hail'd at the twilight's last gleaming?
Whose broad stripes and bright stars, thro' the perilous fight,
O'er the ramparts we watch'd, were so gallantly streaming?
And the rockets' red glare, the bombs bursting in air,
Gave proof thro' the night that our flag was still there.
O say, does that star-spangled banner yet wave
O'er the land of the free and the home of the brave?

On the shore dimly seen thro' the mists of the deep,
Where the foe's haughty host in dread silence reposes,
What is that which the breeze, o'er the towering steep,
As it fitfully blows, half conceals, half discloses?
Now it catches the gleam of the morning's first beam,
In full glory reflected, now shines on the stream:
'T is the star-spangled banner: O, long may it wave
O'er the land of the free and the home of the brave!

And where is that band who so vauntingly swore
That the havoc of war and the battle's confusion
A home and a country should leave us no more?
Their blood has wash'd out their foul footsteps' pollution.
No refuge could save the hireling and slave
From the terror of flight or the gloom of the grave:
And the star-spangled banner in triumph doth wave
O'er the land of the free and the home of the brave.

O, thus be it ever when freemen shall stand,
Between their lov'd homes and the war's desolation;
Blest with vict'ry and peace, may the heav'n-rescued land
Praise the Pow'r that hath made and preserv'd us as a nation!
Then conquer we must, when our cause is just,
And this be our motto: "In God is our trust"
And the star-spangled banner in triumph shall wave
O'er the land of the free and the home of the brave!

America the Beautiful

O beautiful for spacious skies,
For amber waves of grain,
For purple mountain majesties
Above the fruited plain!
America! America!
God shed His grace on thee,
And crown thy good with brotherhood
From sea to shining sea!
O beautiful for pilgrim feet
Whose stern impassion'd stress
A thoroughfare for freedom beat
Across the wilderness.
America! America!
God mend thine ev'ry flaw,
Confirm thy soul in self-control,
Thy liberty in law.
O beautiful for heroes prov'd
In liberating strife,
Who more than self their country loved,
And mercy more than life.
America! America!
May God thy gold refine
Till all success be nobleness,
And ev'ry gain divine.
O beautiful for patriot dream
That sees beyond the years
Thine alabaster cities gleam
Undimmed by human tears.
America! America!
God shed His grace on thee,
And crown thy good with brotherhood
From sea to shining sea.

What it means to me………..

What "I" do to Pledge my Allegiance to my country..........

Music/lyrical credits for **America the Beautiful**
http://www.niehs.nih.gov/kids/lyrics/america.htm
Music/lyrical credits for **Star-Splangled Banner** http://www.niehs.nih.gov/kids/lyrics/spangle.htm
Music/lyrical credits for **You're A Grand 'Ole Flag**
http://www.niehs.nih.gov/kids/lyrics/grandold.htm
Photography credits
www.office.microsoft.com/en-us/clipart
Flag Etiquette
www.usflag.org/flagetiquette.html

You're A Grand 'Ole Flag

You're a grand old flag,
You're a high flying flag
And forever in peace may you wave.
You're the emblem of
The land I love.
The home of the free and the brave.
Ev'ry heart beats true
'neath the Red, White and Blue,
Where there's never a boast or brag.
Should auld acquaintance be forgot,
Keep your eye on the grand old flag